YOUR KNOWLEDGE HAS VALUE

- We will publish your bachelor's and master's thesis, essays and papers

- Your own eBook and book - sold worldwide in all relevant shops

- Earn money with each sale

Upload your text at www.GRIN.com
and publish for free

Mateja Grbes

William Faulkner "The Sound and the Fury". The Corruption of Southern Aristocratic Values

An Essay

GRIN Verlag

Bibliografische Information der Deutschen Nationalbibliothek:

Die Deutsche Bibliothek verzeichnet diese Publikation in der Deutschen National-
bibliografie; detaillierte bibliografische Daten sind im Internet über http://dnb.d-
nb.de/ abrufbar.

Imprint:

Copyright © 2013 GRIN Verlag GmbH
Druck und Bindung: Books on Demand GmbH, Norderstedt Germany
ISBN: 978-3-656-59320-1

This book at GRIN:

http://www.grin.com/en/e-book/268305/william-faulkner-the-sound-and-the-fury-
the-corruption-of-southern-aristocratic

GRIN - Your knowledge has value

Der GRIN Verlag publiziert seit 1998 wissenschaftliche Arbeiten von Studenten, Hochschullehrern und anderen Akademikern als eBook und gedrucktes Buch. Die Verlagswebsite www.grin.com ist die ideale Plattform zur Veröffentlichung von Hausarbeiten, Abschlussarbeiten, wissenschaftlichen Aufsätzen, Dissertationen und Fachbüchern.

Visit us on the internet:

http://www.grin.com/

http://www.facebook.com/grincom

http://www.twitter.com/grin_com

„The Sound and the Fury" is a novel written by a celebrated American novelist William Faulkner. The novel was first published in 1929 and was soon recognized as one of the greatest Southern novels ever written. Praised for its complexity and subtlety, the novel challenges the reader until the last page with its stream of consciousness narratives which require a significant amount of attention from the reader, given the fact that Faulkner changes both the narrative and the style of writing with each chapter. Through the narratives of three characters: a mentally disabled Benjamin, his oldest brother Quentin III and their cold-hearted brother Jason IV., Faulkner tells the story of the tragic decline of the Compson family in a town of Jefferson in the northern Mississippi. Each of these characters, in their own special way, describes the final stages of the downfall of their once wealthy and acknowledged family which started after the Civil war and with the beginning of the Reconstruction. The fourth chapter is written in the narrative voice of the author himself but the main focus is put on Dilsey, a black woman who practically raised all the Compson children on her own and serves as the central moral figure of the novel until it reaches its defeating end.

The novel begins with the chapter written in the voice of Benjamin Compson, the youngest son of Caroline and Jason III Compson, who is mentally disabled from birth as well as deaf and mute. This part of the novel is the most difficult to follow since Benjamin does not tell the difference between past and present: he just recollects things and events in the way they happened, without any personal comment or perspective. He cannot separate his memories from present events; therefore this chapter is consisted of numerous scenes or captions of scenes from the fall of 1898 when his grandmother died until April 7th 1928, the day of his 33rd birthday. Nevertheless, Benjamin manages to successfully introduce the characters to the reader as well as the interrelationship between them, using his scattered and random recollections of events. Firstly, it is perfectly clear that the Compson children are devoid of caring and devoted parents. Mrs Caroline Compson, born Bascomb, is of delicate health and her days are filled with repeated complaining and self-pity. Her hypochondria devours her and she believes that she is on a constant brink of death." It`s a judgment on me.". Mother said. "But I`ll be gone soon, too"[1].She is not a real mother to neither of her children, leaving the task of raising them in the hands of the household`s maid Dilsey. The only child she shows affection to is Jason, who is the least warm-hearted of all her children. Mrs Compson is utterly delusional and ignorant about her children and their needs and so self-centered that she actually believed her oldest son Quentin committed suicide just to spite her. Apart from being a poor maternal figure, Mrs Compson suffered from extreme insecurity regarding her family name Boscomb. She constantly felt inferior to the grand Compson heritage and she had an urge to defend her own family name, especially because her brother Maury moved in with them and began an adulterous relationship with their neighbor, Mrs. Patterson. He lives of their family money and has succumbed to drinking.

---

[1] Faulkner William, "The Sound and the Fury", Vintage 1995, page 3

Despite all of her flaws, Mrs Compson tries to maintain her appearance as a Southern lady she one day perhaps was: "I'm a lady. You might not believe that from my offspring, but I am."[2]

Furthermore, her husband is another example of the tragic decline of their family. Once a successful lawyer, Jason III Compson now spends his time with a bottle of whisky and with a book from one of his favorite classical authors. He has sold most of his family property, keeping only the part with the house, the stables and a little cottage where Dilsey lives. Due to his failure as a man and a father, he has completely detached himself from his family and his communication with them degraded to nothing more than occasional empty rhetoric: "... Because no battle is ever won. They are not even fought. The field only reveals to man his own folly and despair, and victory is an illusion of philosophers and fools."[3]. He remained indifferent to his daughter's indiscretion, which was an automatic betrayal of old Southern values. But it would be unfair to say that Mr. Compson had completely failed his family. In an attempt to salvage at least one member of his declining household, he sold a part his land so that he could pay a scholarship for his oldest son Quentin. Eventually, he paid the price of his excessive drinking and died of alcoholism on 25th of April 1912.

The corruption of morals of this once great Southern family is most evident in the acts of their children. What is common to all Compson's brothers is the fact that each of them had a certain kind of obsession with their sister Candace (Caddy) who can be considered a central character of the novel and as well as the person who gave this family its final blow. Firstly, we can see that Benjamin is highly dependent of Caddy. She serves as a kind of maternal role of his childish and undeveloped mind and his obsession is best seen in parts of the story where, every time he hears the word "caddie", he thinks of her and starts moaning and crying. Furthermore, when he is upset and starts to cry for no particular reason, he is given Caddie's old slipper because it calms him down. Although Benjamin was mentally retarded with no perception whatsoever, he was still able to feel love and affection towards others, especially Caddy. "She smelled like trees"[4], he said, where trees signified her purity and virginity. When Caddie had disgraced herself, he felt a certain change in her and she no longer smelled like trees. Also, when she left, he could feel a certain void inside of him although he probably did not notice her physical absence. Although Faulkner had given him a role of a helpless idiot who is not to blame for his own condition, he did not leave his morals intact. So Faulkner suggests that Benjamin and Caddie had committed incest in the summer of 1910: "We were in the hall. Caddy was still looking at me. Her hand was against her mouth and I saw her eyes and I cried. We went up the stairs.

[2] [2] Faulkner William, "The Sound and the Fury", Vintage 1995, page 300

[3] [3] Faulkner William, "The Sound and the Fury", Vintage 1995, page 74

[4] Faulkner William, "The Sound and the Fury", Vintage 1995, page 31

She stopped again, against the wall looking at me. She opened the door to her room, but I pulled at her dress and we went on to the bathroom and she stood against the door, looking at me. Then she put her arms across her face and I pushed at her, crying."[5] Later on when he was 18 years of age, Benjamin was castrated for an attempted rape of a girl which reminded him of his sister. However, in Benjamin's defense, these events tell more about Caddie's morals than Benjamin's because it is questionable whether he even had any, due to his condition. Caddie is the one who should have known better than to take advantage of her disabled brother and his undeniable affection towards her. It is her immoral behavior that lead to the ultimate decline of the Compson's and even resulted in the death of her brother Quentin. Faulkner had even predicted Caddie's future disgraceful behavior in a scene which Benjamin brought to his memory. One day, the Compsons children were playing in a river with their "Negro" friend Versh. Caddie had soaked her dress and decided to take it off so she would not be punished. Quentin disliked this idea and hit Caddie so hard that she had fallen into the river and soaked herself completely. He felt embarrassed on Caddie's behalf and believed that both will be punished because she got soaked. Later on that night, Dilsey discovered a smudge on Caddie's behind which she could not take off. This smudge was an allusion of Caddie's indiscretion which stained both hers and her family name forever. Apart from this indication of Caddie's immoral behavior, this scene also gives us insight into Quentin's relationship towards his sister and how it will eventually escalate in his suicide.

Quentin takes up a role of a second narrator and shifts the setting of the novel in the city of Cambridge, where he attends Harvard. Although his narration is more fluent than Benjamin's, it is filled with abstract thoughts and complex introspections. He too does not differentiate, as a narrator there is, between past and present so he informs us what sort of a disgrace has befallen on the family from Caddie's behalf. After he had found out that she was impregnated by Dalton Ames, he is infuriated by her actions and his first reaction is to find and kill her partner in crime. He fails to do so and later on is even more appalled when he realizes that his father is completely indifferent to this turn of events. Quentin's anger is a result of his utmost belief in the Southern code of behavior which dictates feminine purity and honor of all men. Moreover, he is convinced that he should also be blamed for Caddie's behavior and goes so far that he even tells his father that the two of them had committed incest in order to conceal the fact that Caddie had "mixed" with other and destroyed her purity. When his father disregards this idea as being foolish, Quentin tries to convince Caddie into committing a double suicide: "If it could just be a hell beyond that: the clean flame the two of us more than dead. Then you will have only me then only me then the two of us amid the pointing and the horror beyond

---

[5] Faulkner William, "The Sound and the Fury", Vintage 1995, page 67

the clean flame."[6] Though he is trying to save their morals and is willing to sacrifice for the sin he had not even committed, his purity comes in question as we get the impression that his affection toward his sister borders with forbidden and incestuous. When he is rejected by Caddie who had already decided to marry a well-off "Yankee" banker, he goes to Harvard, but it is safe to say that his faith is already determined by this point. In his twisted mind overwhelmed with old Southern morals, he believes that committing suicide is the only way to save his family honor. As a real Southern gentleman who is aware of the fact that his family had sacrificed a lot because of his education, he waits until the end of the semester before he takes his own life. Even prior to drowning himself in the river, he dresses up nicely in a final attempt to preserve his Southern values and it also represents the act of cleansing himself from the befallen shame. Even though it can be concluded that Quentin was a highly moral individual, who took the ultimate sacrifice for his family, the deterioration of his mental state which ultimately leads to suicide is another blow for the already fragile Compson family.

Quentin's brother Jason, who narrates the third chapter of the book, is a complete opposite of him. His clear and easy to follow narration describes the present day Compson's with a few insights into past events. Throughout this chapter, we come to know how Caddie's husband divorced her after their first year of marriage when he found out that she is pregnant with another man. After she gives birth to a daughter, she sends the child to live with her family. She named the baby Quentina, in the loving memory of her deceased brother. In the present time narration, Quentina is seventeen years old and surely follows the footsteps of her mother by spending most of her time with numerous men from the county. Jason feels a sort of hatred towards her, not just because of her suspicious behavior but also because he believes that Caddie ruined his life. As we came to know in the previous chapter of the book, Caddie's husband secured a spot for Jason in his bank but it all fell apart after her husband found out about her pregnancy. These turn of events made a bitter and cold-hearted man out of him who is driven only by hatred towards his sister and money. He even stoops so low as to steal money that Caddie sent for Quentina because he believes that Caddie must pay for what she had done to him. Ironically, Quentina manages to steal back all the money that was intended for her and runs from the house she despised so much. Jason is therefore punished for his greed and lack of morals by losing the only thing he truly cared about: money. Both his and Quentina's behaviors signify the peak of the deterioration of the family's values, or at least what has left of them. Turning the remaining members into vengeful thieves and harlots, Faulkner crushed the Compson's to the bone, giving little hope of their resurrection.

---

[6] Faulkner William, "The Sound and the Fury", Vintage 1995, page 115

The last chapter is written in the voice of the author and focuses around Dilsey, the household`s "Negro" maid and cook. She is the one who had remained a central moral figure throughout the novel; she is the one who raised the Compton children and she sincerely cared for each and every one of them. Finally, she is the one who witnessed both the beginning and the end of doom of the Compson`s house: "I`ve seed de first en de last" Dilsey said. "Never you mind me."[7]

Adultery, incest, suicide and other minor sins are not something you would generally relate to an old aristocratic family of the South. But Faulkner majestically incorporated all these elements in a literary piece of work which bluntly tells the story of a decline of such a family and it challenges readers to this very day with its complex style, multiple narrations and a rarely seen insight into the vivid mind of its characters. "The Sound and the Fury" is that one unique novel in which author`s vision and technique are in the perfect harmony, and the vision itself is mature and well-rounded. Alongside exploring the subject of the decline of one aristocratic family in the South, this novel offers numerous other themes which can be explored through multiple readings since every time we re-read this novel, we may encounter something new and never seen before because William Faulkner is an author who refuses to provide his readers with anything less than that.

---

[7] Faulkner William, "The Sound and the Fury", Vintage 1995, page 297

References:

Faulkner William, "The Sound and the Fury", Vintage 1995